Zen Conversations
IN INK AND PAINT

ZENY MANERO

Zen Conversations in Ink and Paint
Copyright © 2021 by Zeny Manero

All rights reserved. No part of this publication may be reproduced, distributed, or transmitted in any form or by any means, including photocopying, recording, or other electronic or mechanical methods, without the prior written permission of the author, except in the case of brief quotations embodied in critical reviews and certain other non-commercial uses permitted by copyright law.

Tellwell Talent
www.tellwell.ca

ISBN
978-0-2288-6405-9 (Hardcover)
978-0-2288-6404-2 (Paperback)
978-0-2288-6746-3 (eBook)

To Ely and Tess

ACKNOWLEDGEMENTS

To all the teachers and pupils who share with
me the love of poetry and painting.

To Omy Romero, PhD and author of *The Boat is Sinking: The Power of Rock Bottom*, for his kind words and support throughout this journey of discovery.

INTRODUCTION

I am a systematic and organized person in almost everything I do, but I have not reached the point of avoiding menacing markers on the pavement.

What I will be narrating in this book are parts of my life as they come to my mind in a chronology that follows an order that has no real significance to the events.

I speak Tagalog which is my mother tongue.

Spanish is the language I enjoyed learning for two years in high school.

I never really learned to practice speaking it, but I got excellent marks for excellence in conjugation.

Trips became much more enjoyable since most of the places I visited were in the Caribbean and in Europe where Spanish is spoken, and I got to practice Spanish with the locals.

I went to America after finishing a degree in nursing in the Philippines.

After completing my Master's degree in Education from Loyola University in Chicago I moved to Canada where I taught nursing at a community college in Toronto.

"Every family should have a nurse." I often heard this said.

It is hard not to agree when you think of the self-giving nature inherent in the profession.

Life-giving to self and others.

I took classes in painting after I made the decision to retire from teaching nursing.

It was too early, most would say. The work and the challenge were not easy to withdraw from.

But quiet moments and stillness give clarity to discovery of new beginnings.

A new vista.
A new door.
I just knew I had to enter.

I was introduced to colours.
Colours give excitement to a limping soul.

I had to face the challenge of what I already knew about me.
I have no talent in drawing.
Outside of quick lines and circles on the board for demonstrations, I have no drawing skills.

What I lack in the art of sketching I compensated with a big dose of imagination and creativity.

And I love to write.

I wake up in the middle of the night to write down flashes of ideas and thoughts bubbling in my head.

I record intimate conversations with God, intense and sometimes bland experiences of the day, thoughts of death and dying.

My INK and PAINT book is the compilation of these spontaneous compulsions to write about what I see, what I feel and what I think.

Now, I want to share these through my poems and paintings.

They are for those hoping to discover their unique talents after a long career of sameness.

They are for those who delay taking action until they are sure of perfection.

They are for those who want to move away from secure organized structure.

My hope is that the jump into a world of new will be an exhilarating experience for you.

It is not difficult to put the image to a poem.
The lyrics flow from the notes.

There is colour in poetry.
There is poetry in colour.

TABLE OF CONTENTS

Acknowledgements v
Introduction vii

Part One

1940 3
Wings 4
America 5
Chicago 6
Winchester 8
Mrs. Peterson 9

Part Two

Words 13
Black Rainbow 14
Sunflowers 15
Nightlights in the City 16
Aridity 17
Surrender 18
Whispers 19
Autumn Winds 21
Spring 22

Part Three

As I Remember 24
Fulfillment 25
Today 26
As I See It 27
Too Wonderful 28
Eternity 29
Trust 30
Good Medicine 31

The Divine Plan 33
Mother 34
Sacred Spaces 35

Part Four

2020 39
Reflections 40
A New Day 42

PART ONE

1940

He was 18
She was 19

I was hatched in a pond where the water was thick with the grime of war.
Where foot soldiers in enemy combat boots walked the neighbourhood.

Where bad news numbed so that they became the staple like the bloated grains of rice
retrieved from sunken containers.

Then suddenly,
soldiers dropped down from the sky.
New soldiers!

Victory signs everywhere
The world is alive
Again!

Victory Joe
to a child's eye tired of being tired.
Red, green, yellow candies with hollowed centres
candy coated gum
make your tongue move when words fail.

VICTORY JOE!
VICTORY JOE!

WINGS

I sail into the clouds
into the vast gateless space

The big bird glides and hums
into the fluffy white puffs

Like discarded old music sheets
songs of the past
dimming as the distance widens

I close my eyes
new images
appear like unarranged blocks of toys
to be completed

The watermarks from the pink carnations
feeling wet on my new jacket
bring me to the reality
of a fast-fading present.

In the big brown envelope
neatly tucked in my seat
is the road map
to the walkways of my future.

AMERICA

The line is long today.
Lunch will have to be fast and short.
But I am used to that.
Hospital breaks
are never leisurely.

I did not take long to decide what I was going to have:
crisp iceberg lettuce with a big dollop of pink mayo.
I never get tired of this delightful treat.
The chicken always tastes the same to me.

Mary is our head nurse today.
She is from Evanston, a suburb of Chicago.
Not only is she an experienced nurse, she is also a role model.
She likes to chew gum, perhaps to cover the cigarette odour from her mouth.
But she has a warm gentleness about her with her patients.
She usually ends her question with "hon."
"Are you feeling better, hon?"

I am lucky to be assigned to a skin disorder unit.
It is a slow integration to new hospital procedures and routine.
The patients are chronic and stable; so are the treatments.
One thing I dislike is the dry skin that floats around
when sheets are changed and pillows are fluffed.

CHICAGO

I am always happy to get the evening shift.
My lunch is my breakfast and my supper is my lunch.

My body knows and has never complained.
I stopped hearing the 5 a.m. wake-up alarm in the next room for those who have to report for 7.

I hear some groans and hurried steps and the door shutting quickly behind them.
I am alone to drift back to sleep.

On Fridays I do my obligatory errands. A quick stop at the bank, or a parcel drop-off at the post office.
The bus ride to the "L" and to State
Street takes an hour.
I need to be back to get ready for work by 2.

From my list I have crossed out the Barbie doll, a must-have for my little sister.
I thought that the last doll I sent six weeks ago was the definite must-have. It was three feet tall with long blonde curly hair and eyes that opened and closed when she was turned.

I even thought of owning her myself. I would name her Chatty Cathy because she can say "Hello" and "How are you?"

The lady at the post office said "Sorry, it's against regulations to send that. You can bring it back in two boxes." She was sympathetic.

I never asked my sister which box she got first, the head or the body.

WINCHESTER

There is no special errand today.
I can get up late. I even have time to watch the early news, and to leisurely enjoy my lunch, breakfast.

In the fridge is some leftover chicken adobo. I will have fresh cooked rice for the girls when they finish their shift.

If the rice is too wet or too dry, or if the chicken adobo tastes too vinegary or too salty from the soy sauce, no one will complain.

We all know just how much garlic to add.
They will know it is my cooking from how the garlic is prepared: white slivers of garlic floating in the dark-chocolate mix of soy sauce and chicken juice.

Cristy thinks crushing the cloves releases the flavour more and makes for a better recipe.

Mrs. Peterson, our landlady, often wonders if all we eat is rice and soy sauce from the empty soy sauce bottles in the trash can on the deck by the kitchen.

Her house has two same-sized bedrooms with two single beds in one and a queen-sized bed in the other.

I cannot remember how I ended up sharing the bedroom with single beds with my roommate Cristy.

It was one of those unexpected blessings.

Cora ended up sharing the queen-sized bed with Remy.
No one dared to ask Mrs. Peterson if she would be so kind as to provide two beds for the bedroom.

We imagine her glare would be worse than her words.

MRS. PETERSON

She wears those dark-rimmed glasses, transparent to allow you to see her green eyeshadow that covers most of her lids. This makes her entire lenses appear green.
Her cheeks almost match the red tint of her lips, giving her presence that much more vividness.

She likes her dress tight-fitting to show off her best feminine features.
Not too slender, she has hips that proportionately balance her torso.
Her hands have the look of well-worn leather gloves.
But it's her hair that gives her the glow of importance:
red hair that has a satiny shimmer in a room with very little light.
Her bangs look fluffed yet stiff.

She knew that we were nurses at the County Hospital.
She was happy to take us.

First day was orientation.
Not wanting to displease her, the four of us huddled together attentively as she pointed to the fridge.

"Now girls, this is a fridge" she said as she opened the refrigerator door. Inside was clean and empty.
"This here is a stove; be very careful when using it. We don't want a house fire."

And more house rules.

My mind was too busy thinking of what to get at Tumino's grocery store to put in my corner of the fridge.

With a little wiggle, she marched to the door and then looked back at us for the final admonition.
"And girls, be very careful to keep this door locked."

Her voice was now mellow, or maybe she was just tired or maybe just very pleased that she had four demure girls for boarders.

I cannot remember if our landlady lived in the house or close by. Like the lady in one of my favourite TV shows, she made her appearance when least expected. Bewitched.

PART TWO

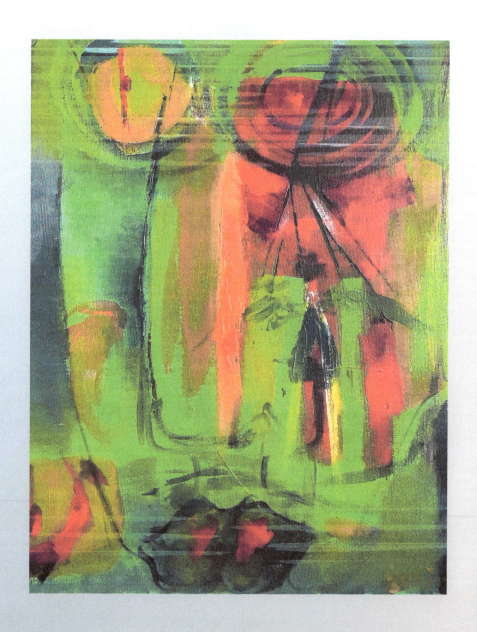

WORDS

She has the character of a poet
She is obstinate

A slave to her judgment
A captive to her passion

She dips into wells of anger and despair,
reciting tales only humans know to tell

She scoops whimsy for a shelf,
releasing the winged horse of caper

Not a lover of order of beginning and ending,
she is the fish swimming against the tide

She sits unfazed, lost in the motion,
not getting up at the destination

BLACK RAINBOW

One, two bateaux
Three four ashore
We were here before
Now here for more

A poem is a poem is a poem
A box of crayons
Waiting to happen
Black is not a colour
Black is a staple

A poem is a poem is a poem
The wildfire of angst
To own and enjoy
Black is not a colour
Black is fear I feast on

One two bateaux
Three four ashore
What waits before
Is now no more

SUNFLOWERS

I fell off from the sky
To a carpet of sunflowers

My body nestled into a thick cushion
Of yellow petals
The morning dew felt cool on my arms

I looked up from where I came
Saw the clouds making faces at me
On the horizon on top of the sunflower heads
appeared a scruffy old man's head

His hearty laughter
sent me tumbling in the wind

His laughter from the mouth of a giant,
breathing life into a masterpiece.

NIGHTLIGHTS IN THE CITY

A tall building wears a crown
Perched bright atop the cement tower
I look up to the marigold in the dark sky

Near and far a thousand eyes of dreamers and lovers
enraptured by this celestial adornment

The city sleeps, a performer exhausted after the
last curtain call

Cars in the open freeway rushing to, rushing from
mindless workers keeping time for the next adventure
The lake in the dark stirs only in the imagination
Silhouette of boats idle, looking lifeless along the waterline

Atop a tall building hangs
A giant marigold in the darkened sky.

ARIDITY

In the desert of the civilized world
I wander

Water flows in ponds and lakes
Rocks put together
To build tall idle structures
Static and dry

People walk
Aimlessly feeling the aloneness of the soul

The breeze has its own mind
moving
unfelt
unseen
the cooling breeze of September

Small boats
Making their way to the shore

A man in a red jacket gets up
Throws the rope to anchor
Hurried conversations
Feet shuffling as they make their exit
The Silence is broken.

SURRENDER

I am sand at the water's edge
Tiny feet make prints as they run
Shells nestle in my bosom
Bathing in cool water
Buried, clinging
Resisting the waves

I am sand in the water's edge
Lost treasures lie unclaimed in
the furrows of my soil
precious souvenirs of happy days
sunbaked as the cool water recedes
they give in and float away

I lie in wait
As I draw closer to the water's edge
Resolute
The wind fans my anticipation
Will it be a bright morning or in the darkness of evening
When the big wave pushes me
To the vast ocean?

WHISPERS

I sit and wait for the moon and the stars
The sun glows red, it burns my skin

Like a soul abandoned by its own spirit
The sky alone lends its presence
Birds fly where I am not

The trees have conversations
Not meant for me

The waves roll and stop
Before they reach the shoreline

Whispers meant not to be heard
Familiar voices dissolve into the void

Why today?
Why today?

AUTUMN WINDS

The wind gently sways the unresisting branches
The pink heads of the bougainvilla nod and giggle
It is October, I say.

Yes, Yes, the pink blossoms laugh continuing their carefree dance
in the Autumn winds
What words are there
That from a thankful heart may speak
of the radiance of the season?
The shimmer of the golden hues of Fall?

Creeping slowly
Into the landscape of trees
Obeying reluctantly
The call of the chilly winds

A few pink blossoms playfully linger
Frolicking
In their Summer dresses

A speck of crimson
On a palette of green
Auburn slowly dominating
The tiresome monochrome
of green slowly losing its energy

The night comes too soon
Why the hurry?
The stage is set but not entirely
When the curtain calls
My lips are red, my cheeks a deeper blush
My dress a resplendent gold
But we have to wait for dark.

SPRING

Like unseen hands
Earth raises its offering of green bouquets

The sea allows its blueness to be adorned by braids of white boats
Tidy lines of boats in the open water

A few flocks of birds hum a quiet tune
Waking up from last night's sleep
There is a glow in the sky, a plane lifts
Its body. hovers over the blue water
A new workday has begun.

PART THREE

AS I REMEMBER

Everything seemed funny to me in high school.
As I remember.

My High school yearbook
Says " she must have been born laughing instead
Of crying".

What happened
That I am laughing less now?

It is time to be me again
Born to laugh

Born to laugh
Not in the fool's paradise
Where cynics laugh for no reason

But in the yard where children play
Where there's mess
Tantrums and yes, laughter.

FULFILLMENT

A blank page
is where a day begins

Each day is precious
It is your story

Make note of
thoughts that inspired
wishes fulfilled
lessons learned

Filter out the mishaps
Keep only what matters

TODAY

Each day moves us
a tiny bit away
from the life that is
familiar and safe
from the constant
that we wish would last forever.

Same confident self
Same loyal friends
Same caring people
Same place of refuge

Each day moves us
a tiny bit away
from the life that is
familiar and safe
from the constant
that we wish would last forever

I shall cherish today
Today has all the tomorrows I want

AS I SEE IT

THE DISTANT FUTURE

Is a place I never long to visit
Not since the days of my youth
When the days were lived waiting

For the next adventure
For the next dream
For the next promise

THE PAST

Is a friend
Where mistakes were forgiven
Hurts were healed
Lessons were learned

The frame that takes me one step back
From the future is Now

THE PRESENT

Lingering moments of
Exhilaration and curiosity

It is not a promise
It is not an ambition

It is the freshness of morning
The cool air
Filling you with expectation
And you shout to the world
" I am here"

TOO WONDERFUL

One warm summer day in a garden
I thought life was too wonderful

When there were people to listen to our stories
When we never got tired of listening

to the recount of the challenges of growing up
to a family where money was not easy to come by

When the school
was a happy respite from work at home
When joy
was given to those needing to receive

And we repeated the stories
Like we were telling them for the first time
And it didn't matter
who cared to listen and who cared not

I say,
Don't get tired of listening

to stories of personal challenges
of the thrill of new love or old love
of the challenges
of raising young kids and old kids

We tell stories
not to be applauded or consoled
We tell our stories to validate
that we are here.

ETERNITY

I look back before walking through the door
I remember the fun of playing in this park
the games I won
the games I lost
I remember
chocolates,
candies,
ice cream,
laughter,
sobs,
regrets
I remember
faces of friends
who had to leave early
Today I see faces of friends
lingering to build castles in the sand
A quick wave swift strides
through the door

TRUST

I got my Christian education thanks to my parents.

I believe that there is a Divine Plan.
That was the prayer.
That was the teaching.
That was the promise.

Not all the steps that I took were in the path
where the providential light shone

Some roads allure
And not always the better roads
But things work out; they always seem to.

Not all the helping angels are from churches
In life there are short stay people
They may give you a lift or they may take you down

Others are longer stay people
Like bees they are good to have around
To enjoy the sweetness of life together
At different places where flowers grow

Others stay even much longer believing everything will stay the same
For a very long time.

GOOD MEDICINE

I see her
A woman
Perhaps hungry
Perhaps lonely

Come close
And see what I see

Not too close lest you feel the burn in her skin
A burn no rain can cool down

Not too close
Lest you should feel the tremors of her body
no arms could hold still

Not too close
Lest you should smell the odour of her fury
No wind can sweep away

Not too close
Lest you should invite her silenced lips to tell you her story.

THE DIVINE PLAN

Once
My skin was soft and radiant
Pampered by my mother's love
My skin was firm and proud
In the haughtiness that comes with youth and
Youthful admiration
My body once tingled in my lover's arms
Passionate and uncompromising

My body once announced its presence by the scent of lavender
wafting in the wind as I passed

Now
Come close
Look at her eyes
A mirror of what has yet to come
Come close
See the rock she has become
Arid and rugged from the merciless sun
Look at her face

A stone marked by the etchings of time

Now
The rock has become a fortress
Defiant and victorious
No echoes of suffering
No memories of pain
Like a mother waiting for squeals of laughter at a time of rejoicing.

MOTHER

She came into this world
19 years before me

As a new mother, she was frightened
As I was at this event

I cried with her not knowing why

I cried when I needed soothing
I cried when I was hungry
I cried because she cried

She had no little ones around to help
No family or elders
Just a boy of 18 looking bewildered

Many years passed
Many tears
Many lessons learned
Much laughter
Many celebrations

Time is never slow enough during good times
The boy became a dad many times
Became a grandfather many times
Said goodbye first

It is now 75 years since she was 19
Sitting in her chair,
she smiles as she catches glimpses
of old memories

She smiles
She waits

SACRED SPACES

Today I prayed in a temple
She was there

She gazed up at me,
a familiar face

I began to tell her about things important to me
such as my day, bothersome things

Her quietness was reassuring,
made me feel at peace

From her broken shell her soul reached out
and touched my restless soul

Two spirits in a space
where other spirits crowd to cheer

where god and his angels
light up the corners of the room
even as the curtains are drawn around

PART FOUR

2020

Like the crisp smell of the paper
I bent down to pick up at my door
The sunburst coming through the glass window
Tells me it is morning.

A new day a wellspring of new
The day will be what I will it to be
Perhaps

Streaking through
The blueness of the sky
There is a pink glow
Of light given birth.

Soon pink transforms to orange
soon a fierce red

It is a new day
I looked at the pencils in my box of crayons
The tips dull with use
Reminders of past new days.

A crayon for expectancy and vibrancy
A crayon for timidity and fear
A crayon for hope
A crayon for love.

REFLECTIONS

The sameness of the day
The calendars have numbers
Nothing else

The days I knew had a beginning and an end
With many curious happenings in between
Not very many of those now

I still see friends
Celebrities of sort
Doctors, mayors, scientists
From the picture box

The names are recognizable to many
They don't know me
But I could be called by my category name
Positive, Negative, Asymptomatic

They need to put me on a curve
That they watch and hope to flatten
I have to remember rules to make that happen.

A NEW DAY

Grey, my crayon today

Like most decisions I make recently,
Grey is the colour

The day seems to unwrap rather quickly
No spontaneous errands
Trips have to be short,
Well planned
Well executed

The enemy lurks unseen
much talked about
like an acquaintance with a bad reputation
you know from people delivering the news

There is less than half a day
Left of this Friday
Transformed
Ever so quickly my place has matured
into its potential
A place to be efficient, productive, creative.

The sun is getting bright
And its allure is strong
I will step out and taste the rays

Like the sunlight you see and feel
My heart is giddy feeling you

Like the sunlight you see and feel
My heart aches for you

Like the sunlight you see and feel
My heart remembers.

CPSIA information can be obtained
at www.ICGtesting.com
Printed in the USA
LVHW071913131121
703047LV00010B/63/J